PERRY MASC

The TV Clues You Missed!

Brian McFadden

BAILEY BISHOPS
PRESS

Kohner, Madison & Danforth

ISBN-13 978-0-9992266-4-3

"Barbara Hale is one of the most attractive women that has ever been put on the face of the earth. I would have to be an idiot not to be attracted to her." — Raymond Burr.

"I remember the first time I laid eyes on him. I was in the (RKO) office, and he walked in and I thought, Oooh ... he's the most handsome man I've ever seen!"— Barbara Hale.

Raymond Burr with the author

Acknowledgments

First of all, I would like to thank Raymond Burr. His generosity and willingness to share his time and his memories helped answer the many questions I had about his most famous role, his co-stars and his life. And it was clear he had a loving affection for the special woman who played his secretary, Della Street.

Special thanks to Barbara Hale's former business manager Debbie Evans, for her willingness to share her memories of the real woman behind TV's original Della Street. Also, special thanks to Veronica Espinoza Paul, the very talented woman responsible for the cover illustration.

I am especially grateful to those who helped point out behind-the-scenes realities that shaped the way the relationship between Della and Perry was supposed to be presented. Note that I say "supposed to be presented." The way that their relationship was actually depicted was a different matter entirely, due in no small part to the natural chemistry that existed between the two stars.

And, as ever, for her constant love, encouragement and support, I am deeply indebted to my wife (and favorite editor,) Pat!

TABLE OF CONTENTS

INTRODUCTION

This book had its origins in my long-ago talks with Raymond Burr on a wide variety of topics, including the lovely and talented Barbara Hale. I knew that Raymond and Barbara were close, but I didn't know how close and for how long until we spoke. I was surprised when Raymond told me that he and Barbara originally met in the early forties and their friendship continued over the years.

Learning about that helped provide part of the answer to a question I had long wondered about. I knew that Perry Mason author Erle Stanley Garner had been insistent that the *Perry Mason* TV show avoid the slightest hint of any romance between Perry and Della Street. But I also knew that anyone who failed to see signs of romance in their relationship would have to be living on another planet!

It became clear that Raymond and Barbara had known each other long enough and well enough to project an effortless, genuine affection in almost every scene. And that affection became a big part of the show's appeal. The fantastic sense of humor that Raymond and Barbara shared was another major factor. Told they couldn't play scenes for romance, they seemed to welcome any chance they got to add furtive glances, affectionate touching and other signs that this wasn't your standard boss/secretary relationship. There were several other factors we shall discuss, that also added to the romantic tension that provided much of the program's magic.

So let's go back together and revisit the show's often overlooked hints, clues and suggestions about Perry and Della's true relationship. Even if you're an avid fan, there's a good chance you missed many of them!

A FATEFUL MEETING

It was February 12, 1943, and two talented young people met at work. They had no way of knowing at the time, just how their lives would intertwine. But each always remembered how they reacted to the other at that first meeting. Barbara recalled saying to herself, "He's the most handsome man I've ever seen." Pictures of the young actor make it easy to understand Barbara's assessment of his looks!

As for Raymond on that first meeting, he recalls encountering "The image of a bright, lovely and wholesome personality whose charm kept lingering in my mind." And no wonder!

Barbara and Raymond weren't working on a film together when they met. Instead they were engaged in the kinds of activities many other Hollywood hopefuls took part in, like War Bond drives. It wouldn't be long though, before they'd both be getting roles in films, and Raymond said he enjoyed following Barbara's progress and watching her growth. It seems obvious that their history together was reflected in their chemistry on *Perry Mason*, and it would have been difficult for the show's writers to ignore.

Even when the writers did their best to emphasize a strictly business relationship between the two main characters, there was a problem. Raymond and Barbara simply never *looked* like two people who didn't have an emotional attachment.

This was one of the key reasons that attempts to portray Perry and Della on TV as simply a detached lawyer and a typical secretary were doomed to failure. There were other reasons as well, which we are about to discuss.

But, before we explore the ways the show got around the obstacles to presenting Della and Perry as a loving couple, we should take a brief look at what those obstacles were and why they were put in place.

THE DUKE OF ERLE

When Raymond Burr mentioned Perry Mason creator Erle Stanley Gardner to me, he called him "Mr. Gardner." He almost always referred to other people by their first names, so I took it as a sign of great respect. After all, it was Gardner who had the final say in choosing Raymond for his most famous role.

Erle Stanley Gardner with Raymond

It was Raymond who told me about how seriously opposed Gardner was to the way his Perry Mason character was handled in a series of movies back in the thirties. I gathered that Raymond had gotten an earful from Gardner because he even remembered the offending studio and mentioned it by name ... Warner Brothers.

Warner Brothers began its Perry Mason series with *The Case of the Howling Dog* in 1934. Warren William was Perry, and he played him much the same way he played Philo Vance and other mystery characters. Actress Helen Trenholme played Della, as Perry's love interest.

Rather obviously, the portrayal of Perry and Della's relationship was not what Erle Stanley Gardner wanted. And things got worse. By the time Warner Brothers got to its fourth Mason outing, it was clear the studio was just trying to duplicate MGM's success with "The Thin Man." Ads for "The Case of the Velvet Claw" actually urged audiences to

"Come and see Perry mix cocktails and corpses!" As if that wasn't enough to set Gardner off, the studio even decided Perry and Della, played by the lovely Claire Dodd, would get *married* in this one!

Perry and wife Della Mason

If you're a fan of thirties' mysteries, these films are actually pretty good. The problem is Warren William could be playing any other mystery series hero (and he played quite a few,) without the audience noticing much difference. Warner Brothers made two more Perry Mason movies with two different actors in the lead role. Ricardo Cortez played

Perry in *The Case of the Black Cat* and Donald Woods was the leading man in *The Case of the Stuttering Bishop.*

Gardner couldn't figure out why a studio would buy rights to the Perry Mason name and then ignore most of the Perry Mason persona. He vowed he'd never again lose control of his most famous character. He would allow other media companies to portray Perry Mason, but he'd have a major say in *how* he was portrayed!

If it weren't for this attitude, Perry Mason might have arrived on television sooner, but he would have been played by John Larkin, not Raymond Burr.

Larkin was starring as Perry Mason on radio in the mid-fifties when the sponsors wanted to start a TV series in the form of a daytime soap opera. But they wanted Perry to have a love interest, like the lead characters of other soaps. Gardner adamantly disagreed, and the plan was ditched. The network created a similar show with Larkin, called it *The Edge of Night*, and had a long-running hit. (You may also be familiar with Larkin from a couple of guest appearances he later made on the *Perry Mason* TV series.)

There isn't anything too complicated about why Erle Stanley Gardner was so opposed to having Della and Perry get married. He said he simply felt that, if the two of them tied the knot, Perry would "lose his sex appeal."

The fact is that romantic tension on a program ... the "Will they or Won't they" excitement most of us experienced on *Perry Mason* ... is often more fun than actual marriage. Think about another big hit at the time, *Gunsmoke*. The nature of the relationship between Miss Kitty and Matt Dillon fascinated the show's fans.

And Sharon Gless once explained to me why she felt an air of romantic mystery was so important on a show, when we talked about *Cagney and Lacey*.

Sharon insisted Christine Cagney stay single throughout the show's run. After the regular series ended, the writers had Cagney get married in one of the later TV movies. Viewers were very disappointed, so subsequent scripts had them separate and divorce.

So, while Gardner's opposition to having Perry and Della marry on the television show made sense, I always thought his edict against any signs of romantic involvement was just plain silly. And it didn't work anyway, because Raymond and Barbara's real life affection for each other always showed. I've always wanted to make my own caption for this picture!

Raymond reacts to Erle telling him not to show feelings for Barbara. Bill Hopper and Barbara give their "Fat Chance" laugh!

PLAYING IT SAFE

It's hard to imagine just how uncertain the future of *Perry Mason* was when the TV show first went on the air. Looking back from our vantage point in the present, most of us just assume it was a sure thing. I did too, until I talked with Raymond.

The show would be an hour-long mystery/drama, rather than a half-hour sitcom or western like most shows at the time. That's what worried Raymond most. Would audiences be willing to sit through a drama of that length? Then too, Raymond had appeared in many films, but mostly as a villain. Would he be accepted as the leading man of this brand-new TV show? Add to this Erle Stanley Gardner's restrictions on romance, and you can understand why even executive producer Gail Patrick Jackson wasn't sure how long the show would last. When Barbara Hale hesitated about committing to a project that would keep her away from her young children, Gail assured her the show would run 18 episodes at the most!

The other big factor in Barbara's decision to accept the assignment was finding out that the leading man would be Raymond Burr. Barbara told Gail that, if anyone could play the difficult role, it was Raymond.

With all the other questions swirling around, there was still the matter of the scripts to contend with. Gail Patrick Jackson was a business savvy former actress whose husband represented Erle Stanley Gardner. Gardner trusted her to represent his interests, including his desire that the program concentrate on the law rather than Mason's personal life. This presented the writers with a problem. Most TV heroes at the time had a romantic life. What to do about Mason, without running afoul of Gardner? But how could they hope to make people think a guy who looked like Raymond didn't have any romance in his life?

The initial middle ground taken by the show's scriptwriters was to simply hint that Perry was at least open to romance. This was accomplished by having our hero put into situations that provided opportunities for some mild flirtation. The first instance occurred in the show's pilot, *The Case of the Moth-Eaten Mink*. In this episode, the sexy Perry Mason admirer is played by Roxanne Arlen, a sultry actress dubbed "The Wiggle" in publicity releases.

Arlen lives up to her "Wiggle" nickname as she sashays across Perry's office to his desk. Playing a waitress, Arlen says she knows him from her restaurant but he's never sat at one of her tables. With his trademark Burr smile and a gleam in his eye, Raymond says, "I'm sure that's my loss." Upon leaving the office, Arlen reminds Raymond, in a breathy Marilyn Monroe-like voice, to ask for her the next time he visits the restaurant. (Ironically Roxanne Arlen was the same woman who played an overly sexy Della in Raymond Burr's audition tape for the Perry Mason role.)

Erle Stanley Gardner Was apparently fine with the way the relationship between Perry and Della was presented. They go out to dinner together, but there aren't any overt signs of romance. It's clear the two have an excellent relationship, but it's quite professional.

Since *The Moth Eaten Mink* got the go-ahead, more of the same seemed like the best idea, so the scripts that followed had some similar elements. To see this, we have to look at the shows in the order in which they were filmed, because they aired in a different order. *The Case of the Fan Dancer's Horse* was the next episode to be shot, and Raymond, once again, was faced with a lovely young woman.

Actress Judy Tyler plays a fan dancer, and when Perry and Della retrieve her "wardrobe," scant as it is, from the site of a car accident, Perry seems more than happy to return the feathers and high heels. He explains to Della that he wouldn't want to have the fan dancer catch pneumonia! This is an early instance of the Raymond/Barbara chemistry coming to the fore. Barbara is adorable as she lets her expression reflect her skepticism about Raymond's motives. Just by pursing her lips slightly, she gets the message across.

It's important to note that there's no sense of jealousy in these early shows. It's more a case of Della simply being amused. At this point, we're just beginning to get to know Della and Perry. And although we can't help but notice that Della is extremely attractive and Perry is a very handsome man, it's too soon for viewers to read anything into the fact that Della and Perry are returning from a car trip together at the opening of this episode. The teasing atmosphere continues when Perry and Della go to a nightclub to catch the fan dancer's act and return her belongings. When she finishes her performance, Judy Tyler comes over to their table, and Perry doesn't exactly resist when the grateful fan dancer rewards him with a kiss.

Della takes it all in, and then she points out that Perry seems to be taking a long time recovering from the smooch! But once again, it's amusement rather than jealousy that we see from Della.

Later, in her apartment, Judy tries a few seductive moves on Perry, and this time it's *his* turn to look amused. Our hero never forgets his duty to a client, and later, in a courtroom scene, he'll convince Judy to tell the truth about a key matter that will save the person that he represents.

Speaking of his client, she just happens to be another fan dancer in the complicated plot of this episode. She's played by Susan Cummings, another young woman who is extremely grateful to Perry Mason for getting her out of a jam.

At the end of the episode, Perry, Della and Paul attend a nightclub where Susan is performing her act, and she sends a fan over to Perry to express her thanks.

So, once again we have a show where Raymond has a couple of slightly sexy encounters with beautiful young women, as a modest nod toward romance, while Della and Perry remain very friendly but mostly businesslike. The "If it ain't broke, don't fix it" motto guaranteed more of the same for the next few programs. Erle Stanley Gardner seemed happy with the way things were going, and the fact that the lead didn't have a permanent romantic interest didn't seem to be a problem.

The next show to be filmed was *The Case of the Crimson Kiss*, and once again Perry's got a client who is very grateful. The actress this time is Sue England. At the end of this episode there's an interesting scene where Sue expresses that gratitude in full view of Della.

While they weren't making any big changes in the Della/Perry relationship yet, the way this show ends seems to indicate that the powers that be were beginning to understand that having Barbara and Raymond play off each other in a teasing way was paying off. They must have realized that Barbara's reaction shots were memorable.

I think that's why we see Barbara showing some real interest, as she witnesses this lovely young lady planting a big one on her boss.

And, this time, there's some tell-tale evidence left behind!

There's a smirk on Barbra's face as she wipes off Raymond's lipstick smear. It may be my imagination, but it appears to me that, with this episode, it would seem Barbara is becoming just a little bit more proprietary about Raymond's smooching on the side. Not a lot, just a little. But enough to spark more viewer interest in the interplay between the two stars.

Up Another Notch

If *Crimson Kiss* nudged the Perry/Della relationship a tad closer to romance, the next episode to be filmed, *The Case of the Sunbathers Diary*, used a provocative plot to push the boundaries quite a bit further. Even the circumstances were rather daring for the time. Actress Susan Morrow plays a woman whose trailer is stolen while she's outside sunbathing in the nude! Naturally, the lovely clothes-challenged woman calls Perry.

Perry promises the sunbather that Della will bring her some clothes, and hands the phone to Della so she can take the young lady's measurements. When Della says, "OK, let's start from the top," Perry's ears perk up. Della notices, gives Perry a mock dirty look, and asks the girl for her SHOE size!

But this episode offers much more than the "cute" exchanges we've seen between Della and Perry in past shows.

At the end of the program, while seated in a restaurant, Perry asks Della to turn over a big check he's received for solving a bank robbery, to the man who had been falsely imprisoned for the crime. Overwhelmed by Perry's selfless generosity, Della can't resist kissing him.

Better still, Perry can't resist asking for another. Della doesn't quite oblige, but the expression on her face as she prepares to wipe away tell-tale lipstick traces is priceless!

While the kissing scene was obviously scripted, nobody could script the look in Barbara's eyes or the smile on Raymond's face. Fans noticed, and from here on out, hunting for clues about their relationship would become more popular than ever before.

Viewers may have wanted to see more interplay between Perry and Della, but writers weren't going to veer too far too fast. So the next show filmed, *The Case of the Restless Redhead*, would include the familiar glamour element. But then, how could it not, since our damsel-in-distress was the very lovely Whitney Blake?

Whitney is definitely one of the most beautiful clients Perry has ever had, and it's clear that he's aware of that. But it's also clear that the woman he really counts on in his life is Della.

She's the one he calls in the middle of the night when he has to deal with his distraught client. Despite the late hour, she gets there as soon as possible and gives Perry a much needed hand, no questions asked. And, when it comes time to celebrate a courtroom victory, Perry wants Della there to enjoy the moment along with his client.

Perry's trust in Della is even more explicit in their next outing. *The Case of the Haunted Husband* has a woman seeking the lawyer's help in what appears to be a lost cause. A close friend has been found behind the wheel of a car that has crashed into a truck, killing the truck's driver.

The car smells of booze and the truck driver had several children and another one on the way. A disgusted Hamilton Burger wants to throw the book at the supposedly drunken woman. Perry says, "This doesn't look like our kind of case," when Della enters his office to tell him that a friend of the woman is in the outer office. Della, whose obviously been conversing with the woman, says to Perry, "I think you ought to talk to her." Perry responds with a smile and a simple question, "You think so?" Della softly says "um-hum" and nods "yes," and the look that passes between Raymond and Barbara tells you all you need to know. Here's a man who has total faith in Barbara's judgement, and a woman who has total faith in Raymond's natural ability to do the right thing.

I found that to be the most revealing scene, though it's sometimes overshadowed by the appearance of glamorous guest star Karen Steele.

There's flirtation in the air when Karen tells Raymond, "Mr. Mason, you're wonderful. If you ever need anything, anything at all, just ask." Raymond gives that trademark smile of his and says "I just might do that."

This was a nod to the sexy trappings of previous episodes, which had received Erle Stanley Gardner's approval. But the really serious changes that were taking place, in a much more subtle way, involved the relationship between Perry and Della. We've already seen Perry put complete faith in Della's judgement about seeing a client. Now, we watch the two of them curl up in the office late into the night, as they wait for a crucial phone call together.

These are the types of clues that were easy to miss the first time around. But you'll find them hiding in plain sight if you take a closer look, which is exactly what this book is about!

HOW ROMANCE SLIPPED IN

It's hard to believe that there was a time when *Perry Mason* fans were entirely at the mercy of television programming schedules to view their favorite show. With technology it's now possible to see the original shows in a variety of different formats and many new fans are viewing it for the first time. They're being introduced to the early years where lovely clients sometimes flirt with Perry, the middle years where Perry and Della seem to do most of the flirting, and the later years where the two of them, on occasion, appear to do *more* than flirt. Many of the people who are watching *Perry Mason* for the first time are undoubtedly surprised to learn that there wasn't supposed to be a romantic link between Della and Perry on the show.

The company set up to produce the show was run by Erle Stanley Gardner, Gail Patrick Jackson and Gail's husband Cornwell Jackson, who was Gardner's literary agent. Gail was the most show business savvy of the group. She had actually negotiated the terms of her first movie contract back in the thirties, something unheard of at the time. She continued with an active freelance career into the late forties, just in time for television to gain a foothold.

Gail Patrick Jackson wanted to respect the wishes of Erle Stanley Gardner, who didn't want any signs of romance between Della and Perry. But as the executive producer, she had the responsibility of maintaining strong ratings. She was a businesswoman who knew she had to give the customers what they wanted and, in this case, what the customers wanted was more playful interaction between Raymond and Barbara.

Gail knew how much Barbara liked Raymond. When she initially sent Barbara information on the show in hopes of getting her to play Della, Barbara was reluctant until she heard Raymond would be the star.

Gail Patrick Jackson

Since Gail and Barbara were close friends, I presume they were both well aware of the way viewers were reacting to the weekly mini-dramas involving Raymond and Barbara's relationship. I also think Gail was much better at keeping her finger on the pulse of the audience than her partners.

Supposedly, when the decision was made to produce another version of the *Perry Mason* television show in the early seventies, Gail was the most reluctant of the surviving members of the original production team. By that time Erle Stanley Gardner was dead and Cornwell Jackson and Gail had divorced. I remember being none-too-enthusiastic about it, because I couldn't imagine anyone but Raymond Burr playing Perry Mason.

Like many people, I decided to give it a try and, like many people, I didn't even make it half-way through. The show was called *The New Perry Mason* and the actor playing the new Perry Mason was Monte Markham.

Although he was a perfectly good actor, rather obviously, Monte Markham was no Raymond Burr. And the woman chosen to play Della Street, Sharon Acker, was also a fine actress, but there was no way she and Markham could even come close to the Barbara/Raymond chemistry.

I like to think Gail Patrick Jackson distanced herself from *The New Perry Mason* because she realized the old Raymond/Barbara romantic tension simply wouldn't be there, and without it, the show would fail. I think she was well aware that the chemistry between Barbara and Raymond was a key factor in the success of the original program. That's why, I suspect, she let so many romantic moments slip through during the first show's run. We're about to examine some of those moments in the next chapter.

LITTLE THINGS MEAN A LOT

Those who are fans of the original Perry Mason TV show, generally look back with fondness on its depiction of a time that appeared to be so much less complicated. Good was good, bad was bad, and Perry Mason was always on hand to represent justice. The other major memory fans also mention, is the overall impression of a romantic relationship between Perry and Della. How ironic, then, that the producers originally set out to avoid any hint of romance between the two.

So, what happened? Actually, I think those of us who've always been fascinated by the Perry/Della question owe a great debt of gratitude to Mr. Gardner. If he hadn't been so adamant about Perry having no outside love interests to detract from the legal and mystery elements of the show, Barbara and Raymond probably wouldn't have had nearly as many scenes together.

Think about it. When Perry was troubled and needed someone to talk to, Tragg and Burger were obviously out. And Paul, while a good friend, was a happy-go-lucky, "hail-fellow-well-met" type. Raymond didn't need "Hail," he needed "Hale!" And that's exactly who he was lucky enough to get.

Audiences have to relate to the humanity of any hero. That's why scriptwriters include scenes where the hero has to bounce a complex problem or emotional issue off someone else to get honest input. Erle Stanley Gardner's restrictions automatically triggered the "Law of Adverse Consequences." By forbidding any romance on the outside for his character, he almost guaranteed that Perry's main confidant would have to be Della. This only served to reinforce their close relationship in the minds of viewers.

And that triggered another "Universal Law" that virtually guaranteed that almost any viewer, paying close attention, would be likely to think of Perry and Della as a couple. The "Law of Attraction" kicked in to deal Erle's "No Romance" plans another blow. I doubt that Erle Stanley Gardner, or anyone else for that matter, realized at first that the chemistry between Raymond and Barbara would be impossible for viewers to ignore. Any time they were in a scene together, it was very obvious that Barbara Hale and Raymond Burr weren't just playing secretary and boss. They just looked too darn comfortable with each other, too in tune with each other's thoughts, and frankly, too delighted to be together!

It was a simple case of "Little Things Mean a Lot." An ordinary scene that looked innocuous enough on paper, could take on a deeper meaning when Barbara and Raymond were the principals. For example, in *The Case of the Silent Partner*, the hapless criminal they help capture is much more sympathetic than usual. Later that night, back in the office, you can tell the two want to talk. Della approaches Perry and tells him she actually liked the culprit. Our supposedly tough lawyer Raymond just smiles up at Barbara and says, "So did I."

It's a simple, very brief scene, but the way these two play it makes it special. Two people together late at night, after an extremely hard day trapping a criminal, and the two of them admitting to each other they wish they hadn't had to do it. It's a scene that takes only seconds, but says a lot about the two characters.

Of course, any scene between Barbara and Raymond was special because they conveyed so much with their eyes. What man wouldn't want to have Barbara's beautiful orbs looking at him the way Della's did as they followed Perry around the office? And Raymond's eyes could make any woman's heart melt!

But it was more than how they looked at each other that gave Della and Perry away. It was also their attitude toward each other. It seemed obvious to viewers that there was something going on beneath the surface. Fans sensed a genuine camaraderie between these two and, knowingly or unknowingly, the screenwriters began incorporating it into their scripts.

For example, they might insert a short scene that included a simple sign of caring and concern that was enhanced by the way Barbara and Raymond played it. In *The Case of the Half-Wakened Wife*, the scene didn't even include any dialogue. Its only accompaniment is a violin rendition of the beginning of the *Perry Mason* theme, which proves quite effective.

Perry and Della have been called out in the middle of the night to help a client. The following morning, Perry is leaving the office with Paul to interview a witness, when he sees Della asleep on the couch. Concerned for her comfort, he places his coat over her.

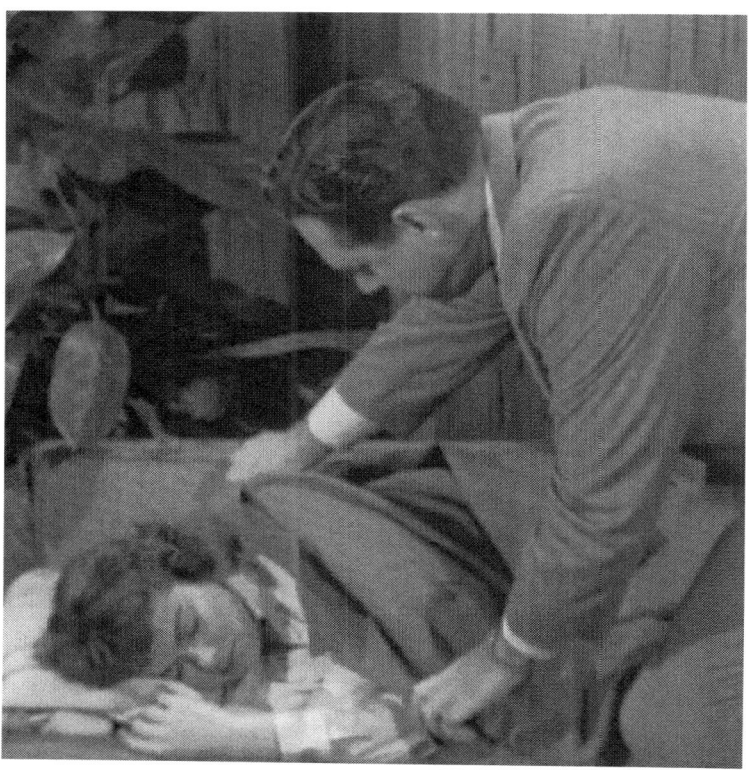

It's a lovely scene, but what *really* makes it memorable is the close-up of Della as, without awakening, she senses what's happened and cuddles into the coat. Our sleeping beauty gives a lovely smile and then parts her lips as she snuggles beneath the garment Perry has given her.

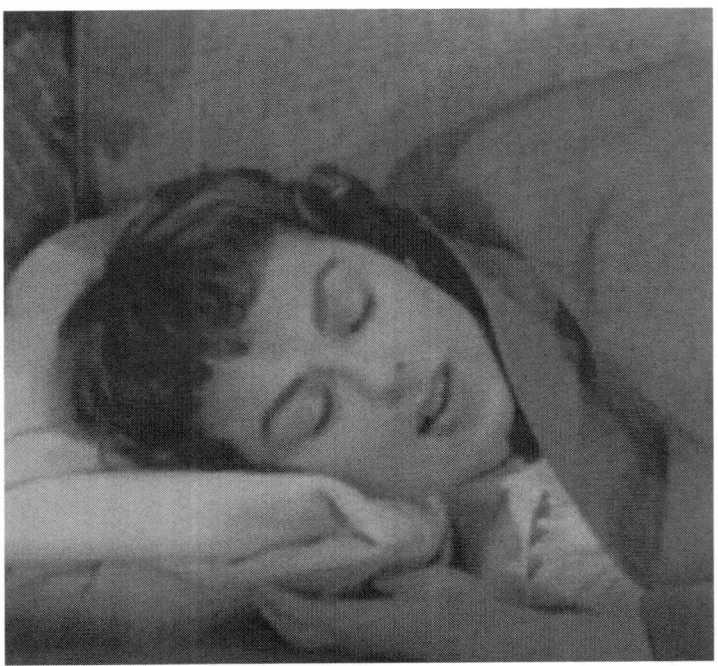

This little scene led to lots of speculation about whether, just maybe, Della's dreams were about a certain lawyer we all know! And again, while having Raymond looking down at Barbara and gently putting his coat around her shoulder was scripted, it's unlikely that the full extent of Barbara's reaction was. The script may have said, "Della Smiles." The snuggling, squirming and lip movement was something extra. There are lots of other examples too.

In *The Case of the Sleepwalker's Niece*, when Della senses Perry is unusually tense, she does her best to remedy the situation. Without even being asked, Barbara sets about relaxing Raymond's weary muscles.

Nobody could blame Raymond and Barbara for the fact that their fondness for each other was always so apparent in their scenes together. But Barbara admitted later that there were times when their sense of humor got the better of them and they enjoyed seeing just how much they could get away with.

In the early episodes we were already getting the kind of playful banter one would expect from a flirting couple, and the smile in Barbara's eyes only added to the romantic tension. In *The Case of the Desperate Daughter*, after Perry helps a female client keep a private matter from being revealed, Della quotes an old saying that definitely peaks Perry's interest.

"After all," says Della, "every woman's entitled to at least one secret." Perry quickly responds with, "What's yours?" With a gleam in her eye and a smile on her face, Della responds, "You'll never know!"

At this point, lots of fans already felt they knew Della's secret, and the adorable way she teasingly responded to Perry's question only added fuel to the fire.

THROUGH THE YEARS

Raymond and Barbara frequently looked back on their long relationship. According to Barbara, Raymond used to say, "When we started I was holding your children, now we're holding your grandchildren!" When I talked with Raymond about Barbara and her family, he expressed a similar sentiment. He had just finished shooting a Perry Mason TV movie in which Barbara's son, William Katt, played Paul Drake Junior. Raymond told me how much he had enjoyed watching Barbara's children grow up.

Raymond had followed Barbara's career over the years and he was extremely proud of her. Starting as an extra, she moved on to feature parts and, eventually, to co-starring roles. One of her best early parts was in *West of the Pecos*, where Barbara dresses up as a man in an attempt to fool Bob Mitchum.

It was in this film that Barbara worked with her future husband, Bill Katt, who used the professional name Bill Williams. They married in 1946.

There was plenty of publicity proclaiming Bill and Barbara the perfect Hollywood couple and they each managed to keep their careers going, which couldn't have been easy. In 1947 their daughter Jody arrived, in 1951 their son William, and in 1953 their daughter Juanita.

The young couple was fairly evenly matched in terms of their careers early on, each making some good movies. And RKO eventually decided it might not be a bad idea to co-star them in a couple of films. The first was 1947's *A Likely Story,* and the second was a film noir called *The Clay Pigeon* in 1949.

While Barbara and Bill were getting better roles at RKO, Raymond's career was also on the upswing at the studio. True, RKO saw him more as a villain than a leading man, but that was fine. He was very good at what he did and made quite a reputation for himself.

Raymond, Barbara and Bill were also in the first wave of actors making the transition to television. Initially it was Bill who made the biggest impact on the small screen. He starred in the syndicated western *The Adventures of Kit Carson* beginning in 1951.

The pay was undoubtedly low and the shooting schedule was grueling. They worked 16 hour days, 6 days a week to churn out 3 episodes a week! But Bill Williams became a household name, and I can vouch for that. I was one of the many kids who watched the show, which had a four-year run.

The Adventures of Kit Carson ended in 1955, which was probably a good thing since Bill Williams wasn't sure just how much more of the exhausting schedule he could take. Raymond was on TV during this period too, and he was trying to change his bad guy image. He told me he was getting bored with playing bad guys. "You run out of ways of dying," he said!

Raymond's biggest role on the right side of the law was in the 1951 movie, "A Place in the Sun."

It was a producer's memory of Raymond's performance as a prosecutor in this film that won him an audition for *Perry Mason*. Without this movie Raymond might not have been Perry Mason, and without Raymond, Barbara wouldn't have agreed to play Della Street.

Neither Raymond nor Barbara had any way of knowing the program would become such a huge success. Barbara thought she was signing on for a limited run, not for a program that would become a classic and last for years. This presented a bit of a problem on the home front for Barbara, but Raymond was there to help her.

Suddenly, Bill Williams, who had been getting all the attention with *Kit Carson*, was mostly playing house-husband, while his wife was the star. Raymond made sure that Bill and the rest of the family were always invited to parties at his Malibu Bluffs home, and he also helped ease any concerns Bill may have had about being overshadowed by his TV star wife. Raymond arranged for Bill to appear as a guest star in several *Perry Mason* episodes, including 1965's *The Case of the Murderous Mermaid*. (Below)

When Raymond was starting the *Perry Mason* TV movies with Barbara (and with Bill and Barbara's son as Paul

Drake Junior,) he told me he would like to have Bill Williams on the new project as well. But, at the time, Bill was suffering from a leg injury.

Raymond remained close with Barbara and her family throughout the years. And I think that closeness was another facet of their real-life relationship that was reflected in their on-screen persona. In the next chapter we'll take a further look at how that played out on the original *Perry Mason*.

STRETCHING THE BOUNDARIES

OK, so Gail Patrick Jackson had promised Erle Stanley Gardner there wouldn't be any hanky-panky between Della and Perry. But was there a way to stretch the boundaries a bit so fans who enjoyed looking for clues to their relationship would keep coming back for more?

The answer, of course, was yes. And one of the best and easiest ways was to put Raymond and Barbara in situations that called for more than the usual amount of coziness.

For example in *The Case of the Sulky Girl*, Perry is dictating to Della late at night, and sees that she's fallen asleep on the office couch. The wistful way he looks at his 'sleeping beauty' is quite touching.

Raymond walks over, bends down and gently wakes Barbara, telling her it's time to call it a night. "Hey come on girl. It's midnight, time you quit working." Barbara raises herself up on one arm, looks sleepily at her watch, and then at Raymond, and simply says, "Why don't we just stay until tomorrow!"

Raymond watches over Barbara

It's a lovely scene but, unfortunately, moments later the spell is broken, as Perry's client comes bursting through the door to announce a murder!

Raymond leaning over Barbara on a couch brings to mind a similar scene in a different episode, where the roles are reversed. Barbara is the one leaning down and Raymond is the one on the couch. At the end of *The Case of the Baited Hook*, Della is helping Perry nurse a cold. He protests at first, says he's just fine, and makes a half-hearted attempt to tell Della she doesn't have to stay with him.

Ah, but Della has other ideas. She lights a cozy fire, and as he tastes the coffee she's just given him, Perry says: "Sometimes you even make it too hot for me!"

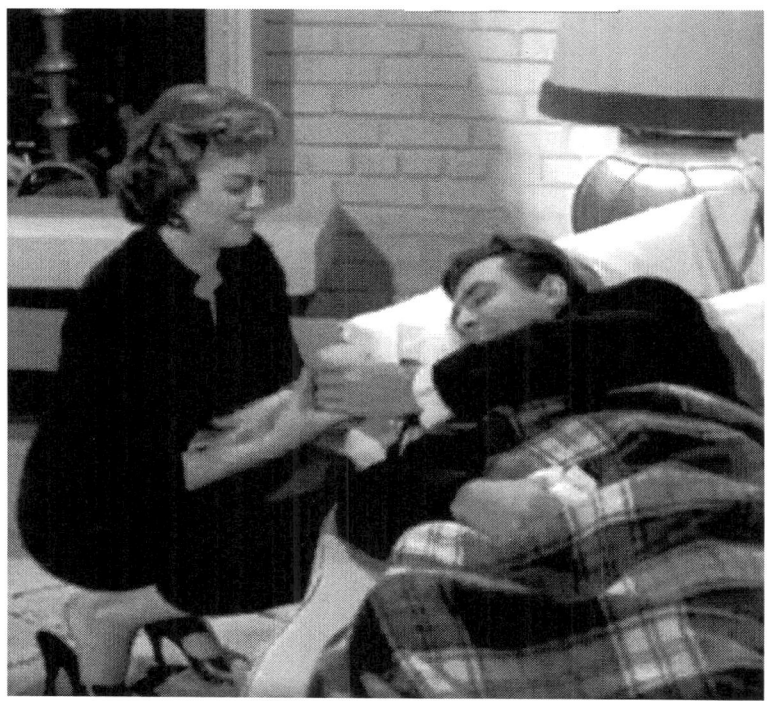

Barbara watches over Raymond

There's a sign in this same *Baited Hook* episode that all of these late nights with Perry must have been catching up with Della. Perry has to gain entry to an office and he knows Della's charms work magic on maintenance men, guards, etc. So they drive to the building and, by the time they get there, we see Della sound asleep in Perry's car, nestled in his shoulder.

Barbara rests on Raymond's shoulder

This brief scene of Barbara snuggling in Raymond's arms almost seems designed to encourage viewers to play the "Are they or aren't they" guessing game. The relationship just seems a little too cozy for it to be totally platonic.

What person viewing the above scene would believe that this good looking couple's connection wasn't something other than strictly business! And they *were* a couple in the eyes of many viewers, make no mistake about it.

Barbara said that even some of the fan mail she got assumed that she and Raymond were husband and wife, a sign that the real affection they shared for each other came through. Watching them made it clear these two people were completely comfortable with each other.

In *The Case of the Angry Mourner*, Della drives Perry's car up to his lakeside vacation cabin.

And, once inside, she seems totally at home.

Unfortunately, it turns out Paul Drake is also at the cabin, and he and Della will be put to work checking on license plates in a case. But it's nice to think that Perry and Della manage to get a little free time together.

Perry and Della get to spend *plenty* of time together in another episode, and they're certainly cozy, if not comfy. It's hard to avoid coziness in the cabin of a small boat, and that's where Perry and Della spend the night in *The Case of the Crooked Candle*. Ever the gentleman, Perry does his best to provide Della with a fluffy pillow for the night.

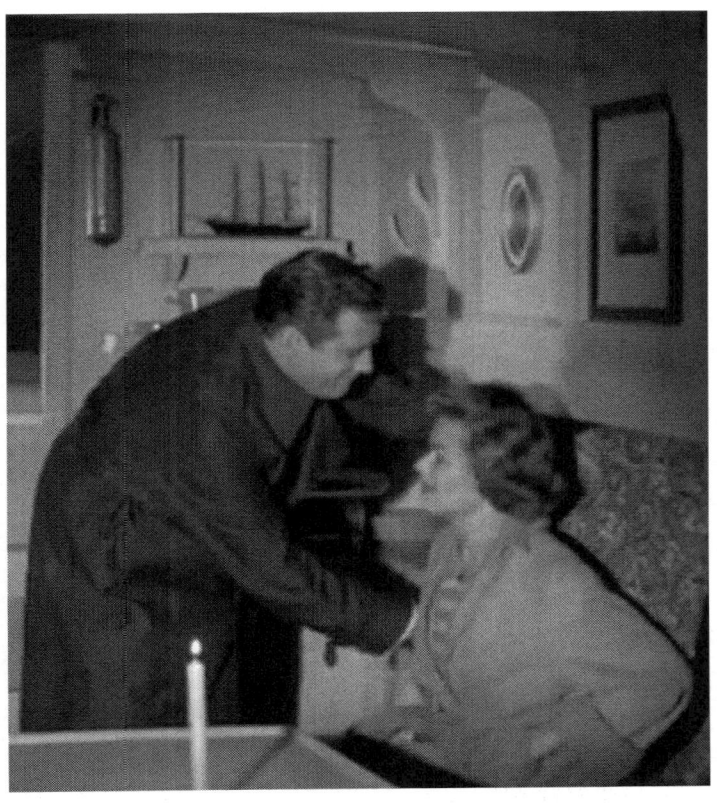

Making Della more comfortable

As they conduct an experiment on how low tide may have altered a murder scene, somehow Perry and Della *do* manage to fall asleep.

Because the boat's cabin set is so small, Raymond is on a little chair and Barbara is on a tiny couch, so the scene may not look all that romantic, but it certainly is endearing. And, since it involves the boat tilting at low tide, we see Perry holding Della close to him to steady the lovely lady he's brought along for this night-time adventure.

These kinds of scenes, however, beg the question, doesn't Perry ever consider the possibility of taking Paul Drake with him on these types of outings? Paul is a detective, he's good at his job, and he pays careful attention to detail. He'd also come in handy when there was a need for some extra muscle. In *The Case of the Crooked Candle*, a large dummy had to be hauled aboard the vessel and it looked like Della was doing a lot of the heavy lifting! Be that as it may, for most of us it was always more fun to watch Della and Perry travel together, and speculate on their living arrangements!

DELLA JEALOUS? PERISH THE THOUGHT!

Part of the charm of *Perry Mason* on TV was that, in real life, Barbara and Raymond had known each other long enough and well enough to intuitively trust each other. But, looking back at some of the shows, it's obvious that scriptwriters, at times, couldn't resist the temptation to add a little jealousy to the mix to get a rise out of viewers.

In *The Case of the Screaming Woman*, Perry hires actress Jeanne Bates to impersonate the voice of a dead woman as part of a trap

Jeanne Bates

After Perry compliments Jeanne on her excellent vocal imitation, she's quick to say, "Goodbye, Mr. Mason, and if there's *anything* else I can do for you......"

Perry smiles and says "Well, I think a....." but before he can finish Della jumps in to deliver a "Don't call us, we'll call you" message to the young lady. The look on Perry's face says he can't quite figure out what just happened. But Della knows. She glances over at Perry and looks like the cat that just got the milk! It was a cute scene, but if you really want to see Della give "The Look," you want to watch *The Case of the Velvet Claws*. Patricia Barry not only flirts outrageously with Perry, but she tries to frame him. Della gives her the evil eye!

If looks could kill

Della's menacing look in *Velvet Claws* was an exception. After all, Patricia Barry was playing a real stinker in addition to a vamp. In most cases, the show treated any indications of jealousy with a light touch.

But the publicity Department sometimes went out of its way to play-up the jealousy angle. In *The Case of the Missing Melody*, after a wedding scene, a grateful Jo Morrow gives Raymond a kiss, while Barbara and Bill Hopper look on approvingly. But the publicity department staged a totally different shot for its press release.

A much more realistic assessment of the way Della would presumably deal with a woman "coming on" to her boss, surfaces in the season two episode, *The Case of the Dubious Bridegroom*. This is the show where Perry finds a beautiful young woman, played by Joan Tabor, sneaking into his office. In the darkened room, Perry sees a pair of shapely legs entering his balcony from the office next door.

Joan gives a dubious explanation for her presence, raising Perry's suspicions, and he promptly escorts her out. Once down on the street, the statuesque blonde manages to attract a crowd by pretending that Perry is forcing his attentions on her.

It's all just a ploy so she can get away, but there's a gossip item about it in the next day's paper. However, Della doesn't seem to be in the least bit worried. She just draws a giant heart around the article and leaves it on Perry's desk. When he comes in, she reads it aloud.

The gossip piece begins, "What prominent lawyer got out of line with a 'Beautiful Blonde' in front of his office last night? And why did the 'B.B.' sprint to the nearest taxi for a fast exit?"

It's hardly the sort of story a secretary would want to see in print about her boss, but Della simply says jokingly to Perry, "May I remind you that you may stand on the Fifth Amendment?" She makes it clear she knows Perry would never force himself on a woman, just as Barbara knows

Raymond would never get out of line with somebody. It's ridiculous to even consider such a thing, so Barbara delivers her lines with a raised eyebrow and obvious amusement!

SOMETIMES WHEN WE TOUCH

So far we've been talking mostly about scripted moments on the *Perry Mason* show. These were the times when the screenplay might call for Perry and Della to do something that could be quite innocent in real life, but could also carry an undercurrent of romance, depending on how the scene was played.

Many of these scenes may well have been enhanced by the chemistry between Raymond and Barbara, but they were right there in black and white as part of the screenplay. Now, let's consider an area where our two main players had a little more leeway. Even for the star of a show, changing dialogue can be tricky. If, however, you want to give a scene a more intimate feel, there's a simple, subtle way to do it.

When it comes to actors taking their positions, there's usually a mark they have to hit. Sometimes it's *literally* that, a kind of "X-marks-the-spot" made out of gaffers tape that they have to stand over on the floor. It's easy to understand the necessity for this, since an actor who gets too far off the mark will wind up out of camera frame.

Yet there is *some* latitude, and it would appear Barbara and Raymond took advantage of it, not to move *out* of frame but to move closer together. Perhaps that's what Barbara was talking about when she said she and Raymond liked to try little things to see what they could get away with. Then again, it's entirely possible that Barbara and Raymond were simply such good friends that being "Touchy-Feely," both in real life and on television, just became second nature.

To use a sports analogy, if TV was like football and gave penalties for holding, there'd be a lot of flags on Perry and Della's plays! Barbara and Raymond often seemed to be holding onto each other a lot more often than would seem necessary, further sparking fan speculation that there was something going on between them.

The nice thing about the closeness Barbara and Raymond showed in the way they related to one another was that everything seemed so totally natural. No matter how many times they put their arms around each other or held hands, it never seemed as though it was forced.

Again, my own belief, and one I know I share with so many others, is that the natural regard Raymond and Barbara had for each other, came through on the screen. The audience felt they were seeing their two favorite actors react in a teleplay the same way they would react in real life.

And it wasn't just the touching and the feeling. There were other signs of closeness that kept turning up. People who are comfortable with each other have a way of showing it. Sometimes it would appear in a courtroom scene. Perry would be very worried about something and Della's body language would reveal her own concern for Perry. It was the same if a situation arose where there seemed to be any kind of physical danger. You got the feeling that Barbara, in the guise of Della, would always stand ready to protect her man.

The office was the place where many of the duo's most "touching" scenes played out. In *The Case of the Bartered Bikini*, it's late at night when Raymond returns and finds Della sleeping.

Speaking of which, how many people do any of us know who have to spend as much time as Della does sacked out on an office couch waiting for her boss? You'd think by now Perry would have arranged better accommodations for poor Della, but in *Bartered Bikini* she has once again fallen asleep on the couch, with her high heels still on!

I've never figured out whether the producers had Della and Perry working so late at night because they wanted to take advantage of opportunities for romance, or because they simply wanted to disguise the fake-looking cityscape they had painted on the backdrop behind the office windows. At least in darkness it didn't look quite as phony!

Whatever the case, working late into the night was the perfect excuse for Perry to take Della out for a cozy dinner for two.

The two were equally happy sipping cocktails, as they did in *The Case of the Gilded Lilly*.

And Perry might also take Della out for a late night show, as he did in a few episodes, including *The Case of the Twice Told Twist*.

Late evenings weren't just a great excuse for working romantic dinners into the *Perry Mason* plots. Since Perry was usually wrapping up a busy day, they were also the perfect times for Della to try to provide some comfort. The hand-holding shot below comes just after Della has given Perry the massage we saw earlier in *The Case of the Sleepwalker's Niece*.

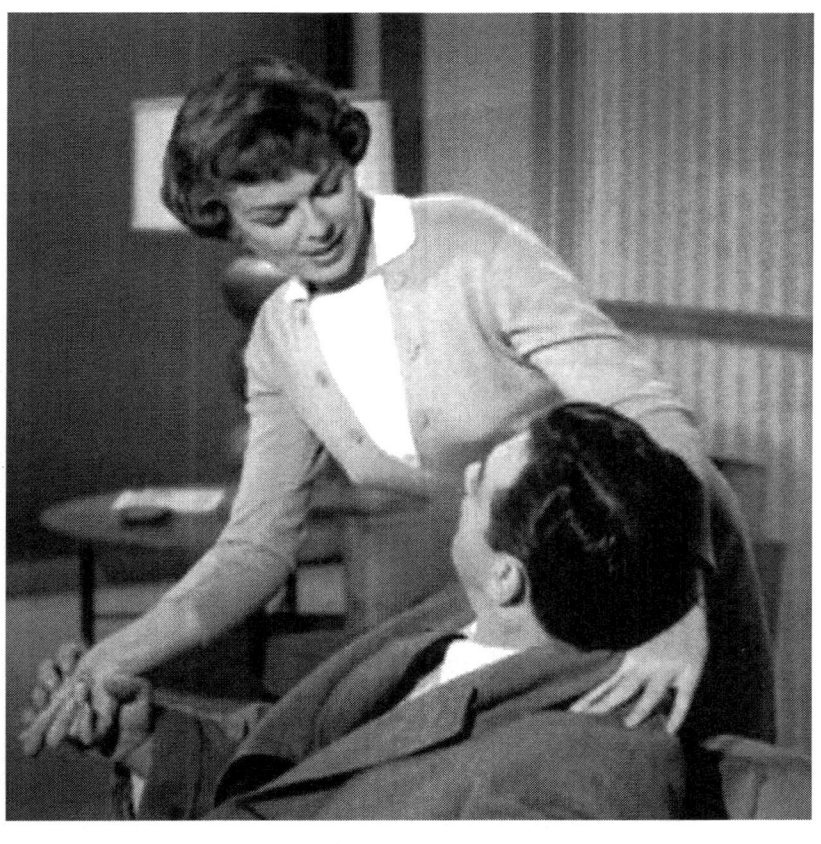

Another late night at the office

Barbara said Erle Stanley Gardner once nixed a scene in a show where the script called for her to sit on Raymond's lap. It seems a shame, because we can only speculate on how much ammunition it would have given to those who root for romance in the programs. On the other hand, it's pretty easy to see how Gardner might feel such a scene was going too far.

But, while nobody ever tried a "lap" scene again, there were certainly several times when Della was draped rather fetchingly over the office furniture!

Barbara was a beautiful woman and Raymond was an extremely good looking man, so it isn't too surprising that situations where the two of them were together took on romantic overtones. And the "Are they/Aren't they" guessing game that so many viewers liked to play seemed to feed on even the slightest whiff of romance.

What fans saw about the two stars in magazines also prompted speculation about their relationship. Raymond would tell interviewers that a combination of Barbara and Della would be his idea of a perfect woman, and Barbara would talk of falling for Raymond's "Hypnotic" blue eyes.

Even the "posed" pictures that people saw of Raymond and Barbara showed them unusually close for two people who were supposed to be in a "business" relationship.

The test I like to use when I come across shots like the one on the previous page is, "If I stumbled into the office by mistake, would I feel like I was interrupting something?" I have to admit, the answer is "Yes!"

Even in a fairly innocuous publicity picture like the one below, it's hard not to notice that Perry has his hand on Della's shoulder and Della looks quite fetching in an outfit that's hardly suited to outdoor sleuthing.

The physical closeness was just one of the factors eager viewers considered as they continued their guessing game about Della and Perry's true relationship. They had plenty of other clues to study as well, as we're about to see in the following chapters.

WE'VE GOT A SECRET

It's amazing how much things have changed since the dawn of the computer age. Several decades ago, when Raymond Burr told me about how far back he and Barbara went, I was truly surprised. There had been a few articles in TV newspaper supplements and magazines mentioning the fact in passing, but it wasn't like today, when information of all kinds is at your fingertips.

That may be one of the reasons that so many viewers got the impression there was a romantic relationship between Raymond and Barbara. Most didn't know of their history together, and without that knowledge, it sometimes appeared that the two were sharing some special secret that we weren't privy to.

Looking back, it's entirely possible that their early days in Hollywood were the real cause of anything "extra" we may have read into some of the especially romantic glances we saw Barbara aim in Raymond's direction.

And it was the same with Raymond. There seemed to be a certain smile he reserved strictly for Barbara, which in combination with those 'bedroom' eyes of his, set most of the female viewers' hearts aflutter and had them fervently wishing they could change places with Barbara.

Perhaps Barbara was the one who put it best later in life, when she looked back on the years she and Raymond spent establishing themselves in the movie business.

"I had known him since the day I first arrived in Hollywood. We were both under contract with RKO, and we got to know each other very well. He was a dear friend."

Think what it must have been like for two young, talented people in Hollywood during those early years. Oh, and did I add good looking? Make no mistake about it they definitely were two stunning individuals. Barbara was being cast in girl-next-store parts, but that doesn't mean she couldn't be *very* sexy.

Barbara and Raymond were survivors. Both had been at RKO for several years, but by the late forties RKO was in bad shape. Barbara was able to get a contract at Columbia, while Raymond began a busy freelance career.

Both at RKO and during the period he worked on a per-picture basis at studios like Universal and Columbia, Raymond was mostly stuck playing villains. But, if you have to be the bad guy in a movie, it's nice to know you're one of the screen's best *looking* bad guys.

But Raymond was tired of playing bad guys by the time he got the chance to audition for *Perry Mason*. And Barbara was considering retirement in order to spend more time with her children. Fate intervened to bring these two old friends together.

Barbara told Gail Patrick she really didn't want to get involved in a series, but Gail insisted that she at least look at a script. Barbara did and realized it was good, and learning Raymond would be the star clinched the deal.

So the next time you catch one of those "looks" between Raymond and Barbara when you're watching your favorite show, think of the Hollywood history the two shared *before* they teamed up for the series. It makes it easier to understand the "We've got a secret" glances between them.

Take a close look at Barbara's eyes and knowing smile!

Ah, what a look. It's almost as if Della has been on a starvation diet and Perry is a T-Bone steak!

CASE CLOSED!

If anyone ever asks you to prove that Della and Perry were portrayed as a romantic couple on the television show, this chapter will give you all the ammunition you need. The episodes we're about to discuss make it clear that any arguments to the contrary are totally *irrelevant, incompetent* and *immaterial*!

One my favorite scenes occurs in an episode that ran fairly early in the series. We find our lawyer and his lady aboard a cruise ship in *The Case of the Substitute Face*, which originally aired in May of 1958. Perry and Della are out on the deck, dressed to the nines and enjoying the view of the moon and the sea. Perry is wearing a tux and Della's dress comes complete with some sexy black lace.

Like a honeymooning couple!

With the two of them looking, for all the world like a happy honeymooning couple, Della confirms everything but the honeymooning part. With just a few words she immediately establishes the back story, as she flashes that lovely smile of hers and tells Perry:

"All I can say is that I'm for more contested wills as long as they're contested in British Columbia."

Perry responds, "I'll bear that in mind the next time I want you to act as a witness"

"Do that," says Della, and then she adds, "Are you sorry I talked you into coming back this way instead of flying?"

Perry, sporting his boyish smile asks, "Can you keep a secret?"

And then, with a wide grin, Della says, "You had the same idea!" They both laugh knowingly, as if sharing a special moment known only to them.

It really is a romantic scene, and even those viewers who remember it well sometimes forget what happened a short time later. After Della and Perry are interrupted briefly by a couple of passengers who stop to chat, our favorite lawyer taps his favorite secretary on the shoulder, signaling that it's time to bring their attention back to the romantic view. And that's exactly what they do as they once again gaze lovingly at the moon and the sea.

Now, think about it. If you encountered this handsome couple on a romantic cruise, would you say to yourself: "Oh gee, must be a dedicated lawyer demonstrating the platonic nature of his relationship with his beautiful secretary, by smiling and sharing secrets with her as they both look lovingly into each other's eyes?"

Putting aside the question of just why it would be so vital to take Della all this distance to act as a witness, the revelation that both of them were so looking forward to this cruise together says a great deal about their true feelings.

Another early, and surprisingly candid example of the feelings Della and Perry shared, occurred in *The Case of the Larcenous Lady*. In this December, 1960 outing, a grateful couple in Perry's office is thanking him for his help. The conversation changes as they're about to leave, with Perry and Della asking them about their plans. Della looks longingly at them as they walk away.

There's no way around it, Della looks sad after hearing these two young people talk about the plans they have. And it triggers an interesting conversation. As soon as they're out the door, Della says to Perry:

"What about us?"

Perry, looking like he's not paying too much attention responds, "Plans? I've got some."

In a remarkably frank reply, Della says, "I'm not talking about our jobs."

Still looking like a sourpuss, Raymond responds, "Well, *I* am."

This seems totally out of character for the Perry we know and love, but as if to emphasize the fact that he means business, he reaches into one of his desk drawers to get a note pad for Della.

"Here, take a note," Perry says. Della definitely looks none too pleased at this response from Perry. That is, until he actually begins his dictation.

"New French restaurant just opened up. Specializes in Rack of Lamb, mint sauce, Lyonnaise Potatoes and Crêpes Suzette....."

Perry cracks a big smile and looks up impishly at Della, who is beaming right back at him. Then the two of them prepare to head for that lovely new French restaurant!

The kind of relationship that Perry and Della had was further revealed in the November 1962 episode, *The Case of the Weary Watchdog*. A close friend of Della's tells her she desperately needs 25 thousand dollars, a large amount of money now, a huge amount of money back then. But she refuses to tell Della why. Perry and Della are out to dinner that night and he knows her well enough to sense that something's wrong. He simply looks at her and says, "Can I help?" Della says, "Perry, how far would you go for a friend?"

He responds, "How long is forever?" Della then reluctantly tells him she needs 25 thousand dollars, no questions asked. And even before she finishes the statement Perry is reaching into his jacket pocket for his checkbook.

As Perry hands Della the 25 thousand dollar check, he makes it clear he won't ask any questions and he doesn't want any thanks. That kind of trust is something to be cherished, and it seems to me, it's a definite sign of love!

While the early seasons of the show contained more than their fair share of episodes indicating a Perry/Della romance, some of the shows that aired later in the program's run were even more direct.

By 1964, it seems clear to me that Gail Patrick Jackson had simply thrown in the towel on trying to maintain a strictly business relationship between Perry and Della.

Raymond and Gail

Much had changed since the show first went on the air back in 1957. We had learned more about all of the characters, but especially about the relationship between Della and Perry. Articles about the show and its cast were featured in everything from publications focusing on television, like *TV Guide* and *TV Radio Mirror*, to general interest magazines like *Life*, *Look* and the *Saturday Evening Post*. Some of the articles only added to the speculation about Raymond and Barbara, even though Raymond went out of his way to add qualifiers.

Consider, for example, this quote attributed to Raymond that appeared in *TV Radio Mirror*:

"Actually, Della is my idea of a perfect woman — or rather, a combination of Della and Barbara Hale, who plays the part. Of course, Barbara is already happily married, and in her marriage she's a good partner who does things with her family. A perfect woman would be like this."

At any rate, after so many years on the air, Raymond and Barbara had been indelibly etched on the minds of viewers as Perry Mason and Della Street, and their obvious affection for each other had become part of the fabric of the show. So there wasn't a great deal to lose by allowing hints regarding their relationship to get a bit broader.

In February of 1964 we got to see Perry and Della take to the dance floor in *The Case of the Nervous Neighbor*. The plot for this one is complicated, with both an elderly woman and her son suspected of murder at various times in the show.

But the good news for us is that our cast celebrates Perry's capture of the real killer at a lovely little "Golden Age" party for seniors. There's music and dancing and it's the perfect setting for Della to ask Perry to take her in his arms. "Well," says Della, "since it's ladies choice shall we?" Perry immediately says "Yes," and leads Della out onto the dance floor.

As the happy couple get ready to embrace each other, Perry's ever faithful private eye, Paul Drake is approached by an elderly party goer who hasn't lost her appreciation for handsome men. Bill Hopper, looking suave as ever, proves he still has the old charm when he greets the senior citizen with a smile.

The lovely old dear reminds the dapper detective that he promised her a dance. "So I did," says Paul, as he escorts his "date" to a prime position in the makeshift ballroom. It's a lovely scene, and most viewers simply remember Paul and the elderly lady dancing when they think of this episode, because the camera concentrates on them. But Della and

Perry hold each other *very* tight in the background. Whenever I see this scene, I'm reminded of a phrase nuns supposedly used to employ when they felt some of their students might be getting too close together at high school dances. They'd remind the young couple to "Leave room for the Holy Ghost." It seems to me Perry and Della would have answered: "The Holy Ghost can find his own date!"

One of the more revealing clues about Della's feelings for Perry came in another 1964 episode, *The Case of the Paper Bullets.* It featured Richard Anderson, who would later be a series regular as Police Lt. Steve Drumm. In this show, however, he plays a politician running for office. It isn't giving away any big secret to reveal that Anderson does win the election after Perry has cleared his wife of murder charges.

Anderson and his family members are very grateful to Perry. Della and Perry are focused on his victory speech, when Anderson indicates he's about to thank a very special person for making his win possible.

"There's someone else I'd like to thank," says Anderson. Barbara gets excited, turns to Perry, and says "You!"

Raymond, in his usual humble way says to Barbara: "A good man's worth fighting for, Della."

Perry is talking about Anderson, of course, but Della is very clearly thinking about Perry as the "good man worth fighting for." And she gives Perry an adoring look as she agrees and says, "Yup!"

She'll fight for her man!

Cute bits like this were fun, but a different 1964 episode went further into their relationship and made it very clear that romance was definitely *in* the air when these two were *on* the air. In *The Case of the Careless Kidnapper*, Perry and Della are supposed to attend a party being thrown by a client he has just successfully defended. Inside the client's home, family and friends, including teenage sons and daughters, are dancing the night away.

But Perry and Della are out in the garden. The party music can be heard faintly in the background, but the two of them are too busy enjoying the moonlight together. Della, looking absolutely glamorous in a mink stole accented by pearl earrings and a necklace, says to Perry, "Are we or are we not going into that Party?"

Perry pauses, and when he speaks he responds to this lovely lady's question with a question of his own. Rather surprisingly, it contains several parts:

"Della," says Perry, "When was the last time you went to a nightclub, drank champagne and danced 'til dawn?

Della gets a wistful look in her eyes and says, "That, dear boss, is a memory so far back in time...I can't even drag it back to look at and enjoy in retrospect."

"Alright then, let's create some *new* memories!" says Perry.

Della is absolutely glowing as she shrugs her shoulders gently, looks up at Perry and, with a big smile says, "You're the boss."

Then the two of them turn, Perry puts his arm around Della, and they walk into the night, ready to make some "new memories!" Now, if that isn't romance, I don't know what is!

NEW MEMORIES

I've always loved Raymond's line in *Careless Kidnapper* about "creating new memories," because two decades later he and Barbara did exactly that, and I was lucky enough to hear about it from the man himself. When he finished shooting the first *Perry Mason* TV movie in Canada, Raymond stopped off in New York and was good enough to pay me a visit to talk about how things went.

He said the first day of shooting just happened to take place in a courtroom. Raymond looked at Barbara and he said it was like magic. The years just melted away.

Twenty years later!

"It was like wiping out twenty years of not altogether good times, just twenty years of your life," he said, "so that you were immediately twenty years younger."

I think what Raymond was telling me was that seeing Barbara in the same role, in the same surroundings and involved in essentially the same endeavor the two of them embarked on years earlier, brought back a flood of memories. They had worked together on the original show and they had worked together in between, with Barbara even appearing on *Ironside*, but somehow this was different.

It must have also been a reminder of the history they had even prior to the original show, when they were both struggling young actors. Were those years hard for them? You bet. Barbara, at RKO, was being put through the rigorous paces that all starlets had to face in those days...the endless training, publicity tours, and posing for glamour shots.

Meanwhile, Raymond faced lots of disappointments before he finally got a decent role. And, throughout the forties he would be a character actor, not a star. Even later, when success came with *Perry Mason*, it was no picnic. Raymond's time was devoted almost exclusively to the show, staying on the lot overnight during the early days because he didn't have time to commute to his Malibu home during the week. Barbara sacrificed too. Her schedule didn't allow her to devote as much time to the family as she would have liked, but she did an amazing job of balancing both work and home life.

So, as I talked with Raymond in 1985, I got the distinct impression that both he and Barbara were very much hoping that viewers would like the TV movie and the network would order more. When I specifically asked Raymond what he thought the chances were, humble as ever, he said it all depended on whether fans would accept Della and Perry 20 years older. I told him he and Barbara definitely had my vote and I knew my family would be watching if the Nielsen people should give us a call! Looking back, we now know lots of other people were watching too. The first TV movie blew everything else out of the water, paving the way for a new series of shows that now provide even more memories for Perry Mason fans.

The more leisurely pace of the TV movies also gave Barbara and Raymond more quality time together. During the first show Barbara and her family might get over to a party at Raymond's house on a night that he wasn't at the studio, but now Raymond could stop by and visit them. Plus Barbara and Raymond had plenty of time together when they were on location for the TV movies. Initially, they shot in Canada because, as Raymond told me, the costs were lower and the money they saved could be spent on things that would show up on the screen, giving the TV movies a more expensive look. But wherever they filmed, fans would show up, thrilled that the old team was back together again.

Of course they'd really been together all along. I was reminded of that when Raymond told me how proud he was of William Katt who played "Paul Drake Jr." in the TV movie. Well actually, Raymond referred to him as "Little Billy" Katt and told me how, when "Billy" was a child, he used to bounce him on his knee at Barbara and Bill's house.

William Katt with Raymond

When people bring up Raymond and Barbara's real life relationship, I always remember him talking about how much he cared for her, how close they were and how long they had known each other. And I also remember what Debbie Evans, Barbara's charming, long-time business manager told me.

"Raymond was absolutely one of the most important men in her life. They were extremely close and she had nothing but loving and fun memories of their years together. I know she missed him dearly as she aged and would often just spend the afternoon talking about him and the *Mason* times. I know he was an integral part of her family. The entire cast of *Mason* really supported one another and had a lot of chemistry."

One of the nice things about the TV movies was that many of the old restrictions on the Perry/Della relationship could be jettisoned. And I don't really think it had anything to do with the fact that Erle was gone by this time. I have a feeling even he would have been willing, at this point, to agree that a little discreet romance only added to Perry and Della's appeal to viewers.

Somehow, it seemed, the sentimental air of nostalgia that surrounded the new TV movies made it more acceptable for Barbara and Raymond to bring Della and Perry's love out in the open.

After all the years, that same special look

Of all the TV movies, the one that probably got the most publicity was *The Case of the Telltale Talk Show Host*, where Perry and Della give each other a memorable kiss. To nobody's great surprise, Barbara and Raymond did it perfectly!

The scene itself was slightly complicated since it involved a double entendre. Barbara and Raymond appear to be talking about a kindly gesture by Della. She's made Perry some hot cocoa.

"Cocoa? I haven't had cocoa since I was a boy," says Raymond.

"So?" says Barbara, giving him one of her rather cute, challenging looks.

"So," says Raymond, as he lifts his arm to cup Barbara's chin in his hand, "I've been waiting for a long time." They move closer together, kiss meaningfully on the lips, and the closing credits come on. It's a touching scene and extremely well done. It's also immensely satisfying for loyal fans.

Raymond was ill when he made this TV movie, which began shooting in March of 1993 and aired in May. I believe the producers thought this would be his last performance. But he managed to make his way through one last show, *The Case of the Killer Kiss*. He was so sick that he needed to sit or lean against furniture during the mid-summer filming and Barbara had trouble making it through some scenes because, deep down, she knew they wouldn't get a chance to work together again. She was right, Raymond died in September of 1993 after a brave battle with cancer.

Barbara said Raymond was her "hero" for making it through those last shows. He wanted to make sure that the crews kept working as long as possible. I remember him telling me the same thing about the original show. He said the crew went above and beyond the call of duty and he wanted to repay their loyalty. How could you not love a guy like that? Barbara certainly did. But of course, there are all kinds of love and all we can say for sure is that their affectionate feelings must have been very special.

Raymond Burr and Barbara Hale added what can only be described as "Magic" to *Perry Mason*. It simply can't be explained in any other way. The scriptwriter provides the words. We have a fancier name for it, we call it dialogue, but we're really just talking about words. The director tries to get the actors to deliver a performance that conforms to the way he or she believes the words should be delivered, but there are no guarantees the director will be successful. Ah, but the magic....that's entirely different. That can't be written and it can't be directed. It can only manifest itself when we witness a special something between two people. And, if we're lucky, it comes through them to us. With Raymond and Barbara we were very lucky indeed!

A NOTE TO THE NAYSAYERS

I've been very encouraged by the strong support I've received for *Perry Mason, a Love Story*. The response has been overwhelmingly positive. But I've also received a few unfortunate comments, obviously from people who haven't actually read the book. They run along these lines:

"What are you, stupid or something? Raymond Burr was gay. There couldn't have been a romantic relationship between Raymond Burr and Barbara Hale or Perry and Della."

If I bothered to answer this sort of comment, my response would be simple.

"First, let me assure you that I am not stupid. And please allow me to remind you that you are confusing the characters with the actors who played them. This book makes it very clear that there was a romantic relationship between Perry and Della on the show, despite Erle Stanley Gardner's attempts to prevent it, and the real-life chemistry between Raymond and Barbara helped to enhance the romance angle in viewers' minds.

With regard to Raymond Burr, one of his best loved sayings was "Try and live your life the way you wish others would live theirs." I can't think of anyone who would want to have their privacy invaded by someone demanding to know intimate details of their love life. I assure you I did not ask Raymond about his sexual orientation. It wasn't any of my business and it isn't anyone else's either. But the idea that it was impossible for Raymond to have affectionate feelings toward women is ridiculous. And it may be that, in some cases, those feelings went beyond "affectionate."

Actress Jeanne Cooper, best known for her long-running role as Katherine Chancellor on the daytime soap opera *The Young and the Restless*, claimed she had an intimate romance with Raymond in the early years of her career. Normally I might take this with a grain of salt, were it not for the fact that Jeanne remained very close to Raymond over the years.

She appeared five times on *Perry Mason* between 1958 and 1966, and she was a guest star on *Ironside* three times between 1968 and 1973. She was also one of Barbara Hale's best friends and Barbara was alive and well when Jeanne wrote the autobiography that included the claim about Raymond. Barbara certainly could have challenged it if she wanted to.

But none of this actually *proves* anything. And that's exactly the point I'm trying to make. Nobody can make a definitive statement about someone else's romantic life, and that includes those people who seem so sure Raymond couldn't have had feelings for women. I know he cared very much for Barbara because he told me so. And Barbara mentioned many times, over the years, how much she cared for him

We can also be sure that fans still care very much about Raymond and Barbara. As we're about to see, that's more than apparent from the number of Perry Mason internet sites around the world.

ALL OVER THE WORLD

If Raymond and Barbara ever starred in an episode that explored the mystery that most fans were interested in, it would be called *The Case of Romantic Innuendo*! Perry and Della will forever be together, side-by-side, with the real nature of their relationship foremost in the minds of dedicated fans worldwide.

All these years after the original *Perry Mason* first aired in 1957, the number of people still fascinated by the relationship between Perry and Della is astonishing. And this interest is by no means confined to the United States.

Fans from all over the globe actively share their love of the program and its characters via the internet every day. If you're reading this and think you're alone in your curiosity about Perry and Della, let me briefly introduce you to a few members of the worldwide Perry/Della fraternity.

One of the many wonderful international fans I've come to know is Veronica Espinoza Paul. Veronica, who lives in Peru, is the talented artist responsible for the beautiful cover of this book. She grew up in the seventies, long after the first run of the original show. So she had to wait for a bit before she actually got a chance to see Raymond and Barbara together on the program. But once she did, Veronica was a fan for life!

"My earliest memories of Raymond were seeing him in *Ironside*, *Godzilla* and *Rear Window*," says Veronica. "But my mom told me that he was Perry Mason, the famous television lawyer who had never lost a case. I also had an image of Barbara Hale in my mind, as she watched Dean Martin leave with Jacqueline Bisset in the movie *Airport*. The first time I saw *Perry Mason* was when I was 14 years old, just one episode on the Retro channel. I fell completely in love with Perry, Della and the other characters and I immediately knew Perry and Della were a couple. But the highpoint for me was when the TV movies were run on a regular basis here and I became an unconditional fan!"

Veronica has done many works depicting Raymond and Barbara at the time of the original series, including the one below.

Veronica Espinoza Paul's impression of Perry and Della on the original show

But, as Veronica said, it was the made-for-TV movies that provided her first chance to see Barbara and Raymond together on a regular basis in Peru. So, it's no surprise that they made a big impression on her.

Veronica's enthusiasm for *Perry Mason* in Peru reminds me of another lovely woman, this one in France, who is Raymond Burr's number one fan. Pascale Sérac knows just about everything there is to know about the man who played TV's original Perry Mason. And she enjoys being in touch with others all over the globe who share her interest. "I never would have thought," says Pascale, "that a common passion – HIM – could allow me to make relationships all over the world, to meet faithful friends with whom we laugh or also share moments of sadness, tears or melancholy...everything that makes life, in fact." Pascale signs her tributes to Raymond with her nickname "Caly."

While Caly is the most dedicated French fan I know, she has a like-minded *Perry Mason* enthusiast in Greece named

Mary Manuilidu, a frequent contributor to US sites. Like many of us, Mary was hooked on the program as a child.

"The first time I watched the show was when I lived in Germany as a kid," says Mary. "Raymond's voice was dubbed into German! Then for many years I couldn't find the show, but eventually I was able to look online. The first episode I was able to locate was *The Case of the Lavender Lipstick*. I remember being so happy that I was able to see the show again. This is the best legal show ever, featuring an attorney who always gives his all to help his clients and isn't afraid to get emotionally involved in their cases. The show stood the test of time largely due to Raymond Burr's performance and the perfect casting of the rest of his team. My love for Perry and Della is huge!"

Here in the US, Cecilia Cipriani, helps run *Perry Mason Fanatics*, one of the fastest growing groups in the US. Why does Cecilia feel the show remains so very popular after all these years? "Raymond Burr and Barbara Hale had a great chemistry on the set and a wonderful, loving friendship in real life. We remember watching them in our youth and seeing the great respect they had for each other. And younger people enjoy it too. My sons and their friends have noticed the many acts of kindness that are woven into the scripts, whether it's a courtesy extended to an elderly person or an anonymous gesture of thoughtfulness to someone in need. The show has positive lessons for all generations."

Nancy Eron founded the "Perry Loves Della" group for those of us who love the romantic aspect of the show.

"Fans have long debated the nature of the Perry/Della relationship. The Gardner books make it clear that they are romantically involved and include several proposals of marriage by Perry. The series, however, had to be more subtle because Gardner decreed no romance. Eagle-eyed fans have long noted the signs that our favorite attorney and his secretary were crazy about each other and the Facebook group 'Perry Loves Della' is a forum for those fans. Discussion, photos, fan fiction and more are available in the group."

And there are so many other great people and groups: Ros Patterson at the *Raymond Burr TV* group, Kathleen Knowles at *The World of Raymond Burr*, and Mara McCabe at *Obsessed by Perry Mason*, just to name a few.

Meanwhile, the number of super-fans keeps growing as more and more stations air re-runs of the original show. Now, more than ever before, there are limitless opportunities to share our enthusiasm for Perry and Della and our love for Barbara and Raymond!

Also by Brian McFadden

Raymond Burr looks back on his days as America's favorite television lawyer!

By the Same Author ....

The story of two extraordinary stars who fought to change the way working women were portrayed on television!

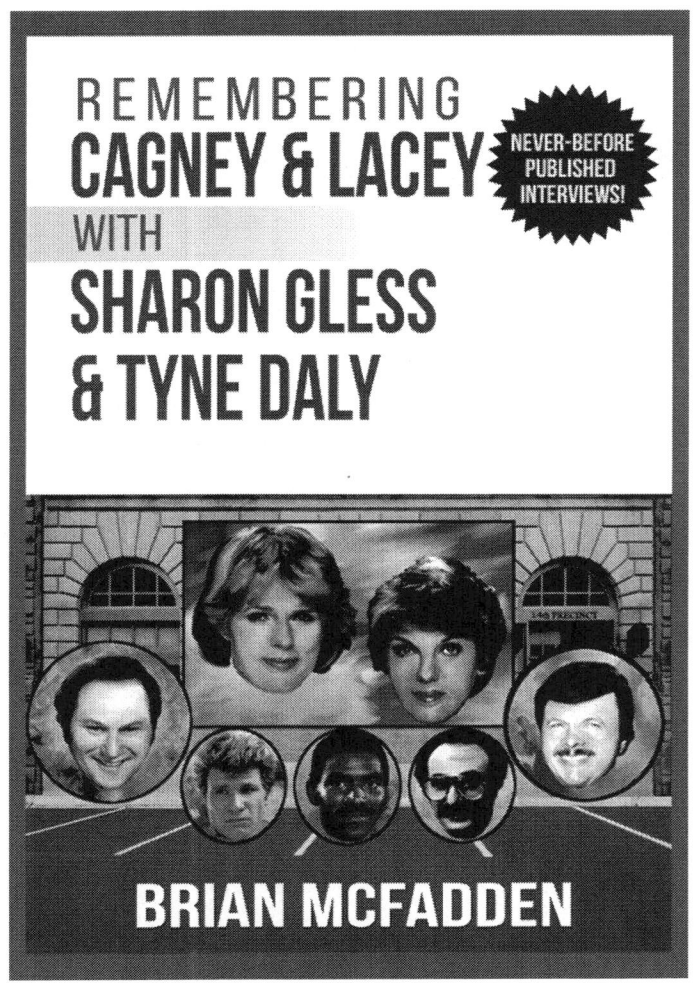

REMEMBERING
CAGNEY & LACEY
NEVER-BEFORE
PUBLISHED
INTERVIEWS!
WITH
**SHARON GLESS
& TYNE DALY**

BRIAN MCFADDEN

Also by Brian McFadden ………

The story of the groundbreaking young woman who produced the original *Halloween* and other cult favorites, as well as award-winning classics like *The Fisher King*.....

ABOUT THE AUTHOR

Veteran broadcast journalist Brian McFadden has covered the entertainment industry for many years. Working for both United Press International and Wall Street Journal Radio, he also wrote for prominent movie and music magazines and was a news anchor on some of New York City's largest stations.

In addition to a series of books on television and motion pictures, McFadden is the author of the groundbreaking music works, "Rare Rhythm and Blues on Budget LPs" and "Rock Rarities for a Song – A Guide to Budget LPs that Saved the Roots of Rock 'N' Roll." The author and his wife live in the Somerset Hills of New Jersey.

The cover artwork for this book is courtesy of Veronica Espinoza Paul. Unless otherwise noted, all dates referred to are the air dates of the shows mentioned, as opposed to the actual production dates. The illustrations in this reference/research work are used for historic and scholarly purposes under the "Fair Use Doctrine" of the US copyright law and are the property of the original copyright holders.

Made in the USA
Monee, IL
09 March 2023

29489951R00063